LAW AND THE LIVING COLORADO RIVER

LAW AND
THE LIVING
COLORADO
RIVER

Robert W. Adler

THE UNIVERSITY OF UTAH PRESS
Salt Lake City

Publication of this edition is made possible in part by
The Wallace Stegner Center for Land, Resources and the Environment
S.J. Quinney College of Law
and by
The Tanner Trust Fund, Special Collections Department
J. Willard Marriott Library

This lecture was originally delivered on March 17, 2022, at the 27th annual symposium of
the Wallace Stegner Center for Land, Resources and the Environment, jointly sponsored
by the Wallace Stegner Center and the Water & Tribes Initiative | Colorado River Basin.
The symposium is supported by the R. Harold Burton Foundation, the founding and lead
donor since 1996, and by the Cultural Vision Fund and The Nature Conservancy.

The Defiance House Man colophon is a registered trademark
of the University of Utah Press. It is based on a four-foot-tall Ancient Puebloan
pictograph (late PIII) near Glen Canyon, Utah.

LIBRARY OF CONGRESS CATALOGING-IN-PUBLICATION DATA

Names: Adler, Robert W., 1955- author. | University of Utah. Wallace
Stegner Center for Land, Resources, and the Environment. Annual
Symposium (27th : 2022 : Salt Lake City, Utah)
Title: Law and the living Colorado River / Robert W. Adler.
Identifiers: LCCN 2023046452 | ISBN 9781647691486 (paperback) | ISBN
9781647691516 (ebook)
Subjects: LCSH: Water resources development--Law and legislation--Colorado
River Watershed (Colo.-Mexico) | Water rights--Southwest, New. | Water
rights--Mexico, North. | Rights of nature--Colorado River Watershed
(Colo.-Mexico) | Colorado River (Colo.-Mexico)--Water rights. | Colorado
River (Colo.-Mexico)--Environmental conditions.
Classification: LCC KF5590.C6 A83 2023 | DDC
346.7304/6910097913--dc23/eng/20231012
LC record available at https://lccn.loc.gov/2023046452

Cover photo: Wildflowers above the Colorado River in Utah.
Public domain work by Rocky Mountain Research Station (RMRS).

Errata and further information on this and other titles available at UofUpress.com

Printed and bound in the United States of America.

Foreword

The Wallace Stegner Lecture serves as a public forum for addressing the critical environmental issues that confront society. Conceived in 2009 on the centennial of Wallace Stegner's birth, the lecture honors the Pulitzer Prize–winning author, educator, and conservationist by bringing a prominent scholar, public official, advocate, or spokesperson to the University of Utah with the aim of informing and promoting public dialogue over the relationship between humankind and the natural world. The lecture is delivered in connection with the Wallace Stegner Center's annual symposium and published by the University of Utah Press to ensure broad distribution. Just as Wallace Stegner envisioned a more just and sustainable world, the lecture acknowledges Stegner's enduring conservation legacy by giving voice to "the geography of hope" that he evoked so eloquently throughout his distinguished career. The 2022 Wallace Stegner Lecture was delivered by Professor Robert W. Adler from the University of Utah on the subject of "Law and the Living Colorado River."

Robert B. Keiter, Director
WALLACE STEGNER CENTER FOR LAND,
RESOURCES AND THE ENVIRONMENT

The Colorado River is not just a large body of water flowing through a long series of channels beginning high in the Rocky Mountains of Colorado and the Wind River Range of Wyoming and emptying into the Gulf of California. Nor is it simply a warehouse of resources for human use, such as water, hydropower, and recreational playground. It is an ecosystem, or more properly, a nested set of ecosystems. It is a living thing. It is a living river.

This may seem obvious to people who know even a little about the Colorado River, or about rivers generally. Sadly, it is not obvious in the eyes of the law. In many significant respects, the law does not treat the Colorado River as a living entity. Some laws and legal doctrines acknowledge and protect discrete biological and ecological components of the river. The full assemblage of international treaties, interstate compacts, statutes, regulations, policies, contracts, and other sources of law known colloquially as the "Law of the River," however, does not treat the Colorado River as an ecological entity, but as a supply warehouse to be parsed out for human uses and economic benefits. It prescribes the formulae and other rules through which we make those allocations. Even those portions of the Law of the River that recognize and provide some protection to ecological resources are largely subservient to overriding objectives of human utility.

To the extent that the Law of the River works to allocate valuable resources in a stable and peaceful way, it also does so selectively. Benefits are limited largely to the subset of human communities that had a seat at the table when the Colorado River Compact was negotiated in 1922, primarily the Colorado River Basin states and the United States government. Notably excluded from the discussion were Native American tribes who lived in the region long before the arrival of

Euro-American settlers, the Republic of Mexico through which the river flows in its final miles, and nonconsumptive users. Some of those people and entities might have cared more about the river as a river than as a warehouse of human goods and services.

This lecture explains how the Law of the River evolved to embrace primarily consumptive uses of the Colorado River.[2] At the risk of oversimplifying for those who study legal theory and process, I first explore the nature of law generally. How does law reflect our basic societal values, and how do we make those choices? How does—or should—the law evolve over time to reflect changing values? I then apply those ideas to the Colorado River and its governing law. In what respects does the Law of the River reflect our values, past and present? In what ways does it ignore or even contravene our current values? Equally important, who made those decisions in the past, and how? Who should make those decisions in the future, and through what process?

Ultimately, I argue that the Law of the River ignores the river's ecosystem values—its status as a living river—because it reflects the beliefs of past generations. Nor has it evolved sufficiently over time to embrace values that were missed or ignored when the Law of the River was adopted, or that have changed in the past century. To address these flaws, I close by evaluating two very different but not mutually exclusive ways we might amend the Law of the River to incorporate these lost and changing values, and to treat the river and its associated ecosystems as a living entity.

Law as a Reflection of Society

To understand why the Law of the River is problematic, we first need to focus briefly on the nature of law. Law reflects society and its collective values. But to become part of the "law" in the sense of something that society enforces through legal processes and sanctions, we need to make several decisions.

First, what do we collectively believe is "right" with respect to any given facet of our society? What kind of behaviors do we want to encourage or prohibit? As James Madison wrote in *The Federalist No. 43*, "the safety and happiness of society are the objects at which all political institutions aim." A century and a half later, Benjamin Cardozo explained, "the final cause of law is the welfare of society."[3]

One obvious example is that we expect people to honor their promises. If I promise to do something and you rely on that promise, it is discourteous of me to not follow through and might cause damage to our relationship. Let's say I agreed to pick up your dry cleaning so you can wear your cleaned and pressed outfit to an important event, and you have other matters that prevent you from doing so. If I fail to do so, you may be seriously inconvenienced and must either shirk your other business or attend the event in soiled and wrinkled clothes. To avoid that, a recognized norm of behavior is that I should honor my promise.

But what else do we need to translate that norm into a more formal rule we call law? We must believe that norm is important enough to back it up with the force of legal sanctions. If I make a promise in the right form, we call it a contract. For example, let's now say I agree to pick up your laundry every week in return for payment (what lawyers call "consideration"), so you have the clothing you need to keep gainful employment. If I breach that contract and you lose your job, I may be liable to you for damages, such as your lost salary until you get another job. We have now translated a societal norm—something we value as a general proposition—into enforceable law. Notice that the difference, at least in this case, is that the initial breach of promise involved inconvenience and interpersonal relations, whereas the breach of contract involved economic harm.

There are many other examples of behavior we find sufficiently objectionable to warrant legal sanctions. In most cases, they involve money, property, or something else of economic value. Other values may be equally or more important but are left to informal expectations—exhortations to "do the right thing"—rather than formal legal enforcement. I will return to that distinction in the context of the Colorado River.

But law is not static. Our values shift as society evolves; as social, economic, environmental, and other conditions change; and as our knowledge and understanding improve. So too should the law evolve, balanced against the competing goal of legal stability. As legal scholar Roscoe Pound noted, "the law must be stable, but it must not stand still."[4] Thus, we change the law when it is outdated or when we realize it is morally wrong, such as laws banning inter-racial marriage.[5] We adopt laws to protect new values we now find important. It was once legal to shoot bison from trains while crossing the American prairie, but laws now ban that kind of wanton slaughter.

The related issue is who decides what collective values are im-portant enough to warrant legal sanction. The key word is "collec-tive." In the past, some important members of society were excluded from that process. For example, until we extended the right to vote to all races in 1870, and to women in 1920, the rights and interests of people of color and women were not fully considered and pro-tected in lawmaking and law-deciding processes.[6]

Under this framework, I argue in the next section that the Law of the River has not been updated to incorporate evolving knowledge and values. Moreover, we have still not included all important voices and interests in discussions and decisions about what values the Law of the River should advance and protect.

THE LAW OF THE COLORADO RIVER REFLECTS SOCIETY'S PAST VALUES

Foundational Documents

With this basic framework, let's travel back over a century to Bishop's Lodge in Sante Fe, New Mexico, in 1922, when appointed delegates from the seven U.S. states in the Colorado River Basin finalized negotiations for what became the Colorado River Compact, the founding document for the Law of the River.[7] What was at stake in those negotiations? The main goal was to divide the river's water between the basin states to pave the way for federal investments in dams, canals, and other infrastructure to facilitate beneficial use (defined as human economic use) of Colorado River water. In the backs of their minds, the delegates considered the future need to allocate water between the United States and Mexico.[8] In the far reaches of their minds, they knew that Native American tribes in the basin would also warrant consideration—at an unspecified later date.[9]

To understand how the Law of the River evolved, consider the negotiating interests at play in 1922. The Upper Basin states—Colorado, Wyoming, Utah, and New Mexico—were developing more slowly than the Lower Basin states—California, Arizona, and Nevada (mainly California in terms of rapid growth and water use). As such, the Upper Basin wanted to preserve its future rights to water from the river before California laid claims to the lion's share under the prevailing western law of prior appropriation ("first in time, first in right"). The Lower Basin states had immediate needs for Colorado River water for growing agricultural regions and—to a lesser extent at that time—expanding cities in Southern California. However, they wanted assurances that, due to their upstream geography, Upper Basin states could not build dams to withhold water flows. In addition, the Lower Basin could not maintain existing uses or develop new uses reliably without dams to control flooding along the lower river and reliable canals to deliver water stored behind the dams. Only the federal government could afford that infrastructure, including massive projects such as the Boulder Canyon Dam (later renamed the Hoover Dam) and the All-American Canal. But Congress insisted on an interstate water agreement as a condition for that federally funded hardware.

Absent from the 1922 negotiations were the Republic of Mexico and Native American tribes in the Basin. Both lacked significant political or legal power to influence the outcome. Moreover, no one spoke for the needs of the natural river environment. Indeed, no major environmental groups even existed at the time to advocate for environmental values in the compact or otherwise.

As a result of this imbalance of interests and the limited set of values they reflected, Article I of the Colorado River Compact defined its major purposes as 1) the equitable division and apportionment of water; 2) the relative importance of beneficial uses of water, defined elsewhere in the compact as human economic uses; 3) promotion of interstate comity; 4) expeditious agricultural and industrial development in the basin; and 5) protection of life and property from floods. The core implementing provisions of the compact all advance those purposes, which were entirely anthropocentric but limited in who would benefit.[10] They all involved money in some way—promoting economic development and protecting human property. They also reflected the values of the Progressive Era. As famously asserted by Teddy Roosevelt, "the western half of the United States would sustain a population greater than that of our whole country today if the *waters that now run to waste* were saved and used for irrigation."[11] John Wesley Powell expressed a similar view, arguing for the construction of reservoirs "until all of the streams of the arid west are wholly utilized... so that no water runs to the sea."[12]

Two decades after negotiation of the Colorado River Compact, another set of interests was added to the Law of the River: the Republic of Mexico. As World War II rocked other parts of the world, the United States wanted to stabilize its relationship with its southern neighbor, which was being courted by Axis powers. It also wanted to negotiate a cap on its downstream flow obligations consistent with the water apportioned in the Colorado River Compact. Mexico sought a guarantee of minimum flows to meet the needs of its farms and cities in the lower reaches of the river. Again, however, no one spoke for the river itself, and neither tribes nor environmental interests were represented. As such, the U.S.–Mexico Water Treaty effectuated a further allocation of water from the river but incorporated none of its natural values.[13]

Later Developments
One commonly recognized flaw in the water apportionment scheme adopted in the Colorado River Compact and the U.S.–Mexico Water Treaty is that it allocated more water than is reliably available in

the basin. This caused a long-term structural problem for the values and interests embraced by the compact and treaty schemes. The resulting water allocation system, however, poses even greater challenges for unrepresented interests. The next question is whether subsequent legal developments, or changes in the Law of the River, embraced shifting values since 1922 and 1945.

Unfortunately, the answer is largely no, but with some exceptions. The major secondary legal documents designed to implement the compact regime largely parroted the purposes, hence the limited set of values in the foundational documents. The purposes articulated in the Upper Colorado River Basin Compact of 1948 are identical to those in the Colorado River Compact.[14] Three major federal statutes authorized construction of dams and other infrastructure needed in both the Upper and Lower Basin to store and use the apportioned water. Those laws did add purposes beyond those stated in the compact and the treaty. The Boulder Canyon Project Act, which authorized the Hoover Dam and the All-American Canal, added hydropower to the litany of human economic uses of the river.[15] The Colorado River Storage Project Act of 1956, which authorized construction of Glen Canyon Dam and other projects in the Upper Basin, provided for protection of natural resources on the public lands on which the dams were built.[16] The Colorado River Basin Project Act of 1968, which authorized construction of the Central Arizona Project and others, directed attention to fish and wildlife, water quality, and public recreation associated with the statutory projects.[17] In all those statutes, however, Congress made clear that the additional purposes were secondary to those in the compact and treaty.

A recent statute, the Grand Canyon Protection Act, does purport to address some of the environmental harm caused by construction of Glen Canyon Dam and other upstream water projects.[18] The statute directs the Secretary of the Interior (through the Bureau of Reclamation) to operate Glen Canyon Dam "in such a manner as to protect, mitigate adverse impacts to, and improve the values for which Grand Canyon National Park [was] established." Congress immediately qualified this restoration mandate, however, by in-structing the secretary to implement the statute "in a manner fully consistent with and subject to" the Colorado River Compact and other components of the Law of the River and disclaimed that the Grand Canyon Protection Act "is intended to affect in any way... the allocations of water secured to the Colorado Basin States by any compact, law, or decree." Thus, even when Congress expressly sought to inject environmental restoration and protection into the Law of the River, it continued to make those goals subsidiary to the compact's water apportionment scheme.

In the decades following adoption of most aspects of the Law of the River, Congress also enacted generic environmental protection statutes such as the National Environmental Policy Act and the Endangered Species Act.[19] In theory, these statutes could override aspects of the Law of the River that contravened environmental restoration and protection goals. In another context, however, the U.S. Supreme Court ruled that those statutes only apply to discre-tionary agency action.[20] Following this precedent, a federal appellate court ruled that the compact and other components of the Law of the River imposed nondiscretionary requirements that overrode later-enacted environmental laws.[21]

Returning to the opening theme, the Law of the River has not evolved significantly enough to reflect our current understanding of the Colorado River as a living entity and to embrace our evolving values that such places deserve protection. The Colorado River Compact and the early twentieth-century values it reflects continue to reign supreme. The next task is to ascertain the impact of this legal regime on the river and its users.

Impacts on Colorado River Ecosystems

To implement the major provisions of the compact and treaty, both the Lower and Upper Basin states needed massive infrastructure to "control" the volatile hydrologic giant that was the natural Colo-rado River system. The Hoover Dam and a series of smaller dams along the lower reaches of the river in the United States stored water for use when needed. The dams, along with levees, artificially armored banks, and channelization also controlled massive periodic seasonal spring floods. The river's floods continuously reshaped the natural system, thereby providing new and refreshed habitats. But flooding also destroyed human structures, including artificial diversions built for irrigation and other uses. Given that the river did not flow through the areas of greatest water need, such as California's Imperial Valley, the Lower Basin also required new diversions such as the All-American Canal.[22]

To fulfill its compact responsibilities and to store and deliver water for its own use, the Upper Basin in turn needed its own dams and related diversion structures. Glen Canyon Dam was the largest and most important dam to ensure that the Upper Basin could meet its downstream delivery obligations. Other dams, such as Flaming Gorge in northeastern Utah, a series of dams in southwestern Colorado, and New Mexico's Navajo Dam, helped the Upper Basin states store water for irrigation and other uses.

By some measures this massive set of dams and infrastructure altered the hydrology and other physical features of the Colorado River system more than any other major river in the world at the time.[23] The reservoirs inundated large amounts of riparian habitat, transforming long stretches of flowing river into artificial lakes. Huge water depletions left less water in the river for native fish species and the inability to support riparian and floodplain ecosystems and the species that depended on them. The dams fundamentally changed the river's annual flow patterns, further affecting natural sloughs, riparian wetlands, and sandbars that formed natural spawning and rearing habitat for native fish. The dams also interrupted the natural flow of sediment and biotic material, which shaped the river's riparian habitats and provided nutrients and other food for multiple trophic levels. Non-native species now dominate some river reaches and large portions of riparian habitat. These changes have caused or contributed to the extirpation of some native species and threatened or endangered others, including fish, plants, and birds.

We have not ignored the impacts of Colorado River development entirely. In the past several decades, in part prodded by the Endangered Species Act, the Grand Canyon Protection Act, and other legal requirements, agencies and collaborators have planned and implemented restoration programs along major river reaches. Those include the Upper Colorado River Endangered Fish Recovery Program, the San Juan River Basin Recovery Implementation Program, the Glen Canyon Dam Adaptive Management Program, the Lower Colorado River Multi-Species Conservation Program, and collaboration with Mexico to restore the Colorado River delta. More localized restoration projects occur elsewhere along the river corridor.

These efforts have been effective to varying degrees but are limited by the existing legal framework and the dams and other infrastructure that have fundamentally changed much of the natural river system. One major example will illustrate the nature and magnitude of the challenges. As one sign of progress, in 2021 the U.S. Fish and Wildlife Service (FWS) revised the Endangered Species Act listing designation for Humpback chub from endangered to threatened.[24] That is very good news, but we also need to put it into perspective.

First, the criteria FWS established for this "down listing" included redundant adult Humpback subpopulations of sufficient size to be self-sustaining, and to be able to repopulate other subpopulations in the event of a decline due to either variable natural conditions or artificial threats. There are now six subpopulations of adult Humpback chub—again, good news. However, as of a recent (2018) FWS status assessment, most of the fish (roughly 12,000 out of 16,000) are in a single subpopulation in the Grand Canyon. Other subpopulations barely meet the target size for down listing, meaning the overall metapopulation of Humpbacks remains vulnerable.[25]

In addition, Colorado River conditions remain fundamentally changed in ways that make it challenging to make more progress, or even to reliably maintain the progress made thus far. Non-native fish species continue to dominate large portions of the river, outcompeting and sometimes preying on native fish. The river's annual flow pattern remains dramatically changed from that in which native fish and other species evolved. The pre-dam river experienced a volatile annual fluctuation from intense spring floods to a trickle by late summer and fall, shaping and reshaping the habitats relied on by native species. The post-dam river has a comparatively constant flow—more predictable for human use but inconsistent with the habitat needs of native fish. The dams have also significantly changed the river's temperature regime and sediment load in which native fish evolved to thrive.[26]

Climate change also significantly alters the river and its ecosystems. As precipitation patterns have changed in Colorado River Basin mountains, and as rising temperatures have changed the amount of runoff that reaches the river, water levels and reservoir storage have declined significantly. Experts predict that even greater shortages are likely in the coming decades, meaning less water for both human and natural uses, and even greater threats to Colorado River ecosystems.[27]

As a result of these significant changes, FWS highlights considerable uncertainty about the fate of Humpback populations in the coming decades, with a range of possible predictions from bad to good outcomes.[28] But Humpback chub is only one example of species adversely affected by anthropomorphic changes in the Colorado River ecosystem. Unlike the down listing of the Humpback chub, for example, FWS declined to take similar action for the southwestern willow flycatcher from endangered status.[29] And impacts to individual species are only one indicator of loss of ecosystem structure and function, although an ethically and legally significant one.

In short, an overall assessment of efforts to protect and restore Colorado River ecosystems from the dramatic changes to structure and function is that we have perhaps stemmed the bleeding, but we have not restored the patient's full health. Thus far, we have used a geographically fragmented rather than a basin-wide approach to river restoration. In some key respects—particularly restoration of natural flow patterns—those efforts have been sporadic rather than ongoing. This is true in large part because restoration efforts are constrained by the dams and other physical infrastructure in the basin, and most significantly by the legal primacy of the Law of the River. Of those two limiting factors, it is easier to change the law than to remove the dams. The key question is how we might expand the values addressed in the Law of the River to better protect the river as a living entity as well as preserve its economic worth. The remainder of this lecture will address two possible ways to do so.

The Law of the River: Aspirations for the Future

Two potential approaches might expand the values protected by the Law of the River in ways that more properly balance the river's economic value to people and the river's worth as a living entity. The first—embracing and applying the growing "rights of nature" movement to afford legal rights to nonhuman living things—would most appropriately recognize the intrinsic values of the Colorado River and its ecosystems. Given the current state of rights of nature law in the United States, however, this approach is aspirational but probably unrealistic in the short term. The second approach, amending the Colorado River Compact to reflect environmental as well as economic goals, faces political obstacles but is more feasible in a meaningful time frame.

Rights of Nature

Rights of nature theory suggests that non-human components of nature—such as species or ecosystems—have rights that deserve legal recognition and protection. This is a controversial proposition, but it has deep roots in environmental discourse. Legal philosopher Christopher D. Stone invoked the idea beginning in the early 1970s:

> Throughout legal history, each successive extension of rights to some new entity has been, theretofore, a bit unthinkable. . . .

I am quite seriously proposing that we give legal rights to forests, oceans, rivers, and other so-called "natural objects" in the environment—indeed, to the natural environment as a whole.[30]

But the idea can be traced back even further. Aldo Leopold expressed similar views in his seminal work of environmental ethics, *A Sand County Almanac*:

> Odysseus… hanged all on one rope a dozen slave-girls of his household whom he suspected of misbehaving…. The girls were property. The disposal of property was then, as now, a matter of expediency, not right or wrong. There is yet no ethic dealing with man's relation to land and to the animals and plants which grow upon it. Land, like Odysseus' slave-girls, is still property. The land-relation is still strictly economic.[31]

By referring to land and a land ethic, Leopold likely did not intend to exclude water and aquatic ecosystems. Under his view, it is ethically wrong to treat the Colorado River as no more than economic property to use and dispose of as we wish, with no consideration of the river's inherent rights to exist and thrive.

It is easy to state such rights of nature conceptually, but the idea raises challenging legal sub-issues. To what "level" of nature should the concept apply, that is, to individual animals, subpopulations, species, ecosystem components (such as rivers or lakes), or all the above? Nature can be subdivided in many ways, and for many purposes. Even if we continue to debate the scope and meaning of human rights, we have clear frameworks for identifying the kinds of rights that apply to people, such as the Bill of Rights in the U.S. Constitution and the Universal Declaration of Human Rights internationally.[32] What kinds of legally recognizable rights apply to components of nature, and how should they be applied? Moreover, even the most sentient components of nature cannot use human language to express their needs and preferences. Thus, beyond Dr. Seuss's fictional Lorax,[33] who has authority—not to mention sufficient wisdom—to represent nature in court and to vindicate its interests?

Despite these practical and conceptual challenges, there is growing precedent to recognize rights of nature around the world.[34] The Ecuadorian Constitution ratifies rights of nature that have been recognized by Indigenous people in that region for centuries.[35] Applying that provision to the Vilcabamba River, an Ecuadorian court ruled that the right requires precautionary measures before embarking on development projects that might affect the river's health and shifts the burden of proof to polluters to demonstrate an absence of significant harm.[36] New Zealand has granted legal rights to some natural systems by statute. For example, the 2017 Te Awa Tupua Act grants the Whanganui River the "rights, duties, powers, and liabilities of a legal person." It also designates guardians to act as landowners of the riverbed (similar to U.S. public trust law) and to act and speak on behalf of the river.[37] This latter provision addresses the "who speaks for the trees" problem posed in *The Lorax*, and more seriously in Stone's *Should Trees Have Standing?* More recently, recognition and protection of rights of nature have been advocated at the international level through a proposed Universal Declaration of the Rights of Nature.

Despite these applications of rights of nature in other countries, however, the idea has had considerably less traction in the United States. Some localities and tribes have adopted ordinances recognizing rights for components of nature, but the concept has not received judicial acceptance. Indeed, a lawsuit seeking legal rights for the Colorado River was withdrawn in the face of threatened disciplinary action against the attorney who filed the case.[38] A significant barrier to the concept is the prevailing law of legal standing to sue in U.S. courts, which limits the ability of humans to take legal action purely on behalf of natural objects—as opposed to lawsuits seeking to vindicate human uses of nature for their own benefit or enjoyment. Indeed, the U.S. Supreme Court rejected Christopher Stone's idea that "trees have standing" in the seminal 1972 case of *Sierra Club v. Morton*, although with a famous dissent by Justice William O. Douglas arguing the merits of Stone's thesis.[39]

Short of constitutional amendments at the national or state levels, therefore, it seems unlikely that the ecosystem and other natural values of the Colorado River will receive greater protection through rights of nature theory. A more immediately feasible solution, then, would be to amend the Colorado River Compact to recognize the environmental values of the river and its ecosystems, and to afford them protection balanced against the existing anthropocentric values promoted by the Law of the River.

Amending the Colorado River Compact: Lessons from Transboundary Water Law

As discussed earlier, the 1922 Colorado River Compact embraces human but not ecosystem values. Fortunately, international transboundary water law provides concepts and precedent for the kinds of amendments to the Colorado River Compact that might provide an appropriate balance between the river's ecosystem values and its utility for human economic use. Some useful models include the 1992 Convention on the Protection and Use of Transboundary Watercourses and International Lakes (the *Water Convention*), the 1997 Convention on the Law of the Non-Navigational Uses of International Watercourses (the *International Watercourses Convention*), and the 1997 Model Water Compact proposed by the Utton Transboundary Resources Center at the University of New Mexico (the *Model Water Compact*).[40]

Although there are many ways the Colorado River Compact might be amended to better embrace environmental values, I will propose five examples as a starting point for consideration. For each proposal, I will present first the analogous provision in a transboundary water law model and then propose specific amendments to the compact.

First, the compact should be amended to add environmental restoration goals to the existing list of human-centered goals. The

Water Convention includes goals to "ensure that transboundary waters are used with the aim of ecologically sound and rational water management, conservation of water resources and environmental protection" and to "ensure conservation and, where necessary, restoration of ecosystems." Two amendments to the compact could promote similar ends. Compact Article I could be amended to add: "to restore and protect the fish, wildlife, and other environmental resources of the Colorado River system and its ecosystems" to the list of compact goals. The existing goal to promote "the storage of its waters" could also be amended to "the conservation and storage of its waters."

Second, simply articulating environmental goals will not ensure that they will receive equal attention, especially given the institutional inertia inherent in a century-long history of maximizing human uses of the river. The *International Watercourses Convention* addresses this issue by providing: "The weight to be given to each factor is to be determined by its importance in comparison with that of other relevant factors... all relevant factors are to be considered together and a conclusion reached on the basis of the whole." A similar provision could be included in the compact, such as: "The water use and allocation provisions of this compact shall be implemented in ways that provide equal consideration to its basin-wide conservation, restoration, and protection provisions."

Third, including environmental goals in the compact is not likely to produce effective environmental restoration and protection absent an institutional entity with sufficient jurisdiction and authority to effectuate those goals. Currently, no single entity is charged with management of the entire Colorado River watershed with consideration of a full range of values and goals that would be included in an amended compact. This is notably different from similar large watersheds in the United States that benefit from management by umbrella organizations such as the Chesapeake Bay Commission or the Great Lakes Commission. The *International Watercourses Convention* encourages "joint mechanisms or commissions" to promote and implement comprehensive, collaborative, basin-wide management and protection. The Colorado River Compact could be amended to create a Colorado River Commission charged with designing and implementing basin-wide environmental restoration and protection programs. Ideally, the commission should include balanced representation from federal and state governments in Mexico as well as the United States, tribal governments, and both consumptive and non-consumptive river interests (including water, power, recreation, and environmental representatives).

Fourth, it will be challenging to properly balance vague environmental goals with the compact's more utilitarian goals when the latter include specific operational provisions as well as aspirations. *The Model Water Compact* suggests that states or interstate bodies define minimum instream flows to maintain "a healthy and productive Basinwide ecosystem in designated reaches of the system." Article II of the Colorado River Compact could be amended to require the new basin-wide commission to "develop and meet targets for instream flow volumes and timing to restore and protect the river's ecosystems." Particularly as river and reservoir levels decline, it will ensure that enough water remains in the natural system to support an agreed-upon maintenance level of ecosystem structure and function.

Fifth, the *International Watercourses Convention* provides that states "shall, individually and, where appropriate, jointly, protect and preserve the ecosystems of international watercourses." Such environmental goals cannot be achieved as long as the compact continues to reflect a nineteenth-century understanding of the term "beneficial use." In particular, the compact currently provides that "the States of the Upper Division shall not withhold water, and the States of the Lower Division shall not require the delivery of water, which cannot reasonably be applied to beneficial use." This limitation could be minimized or eliminated by expanding the compact's definition of beneficial use to include restoration and maintenance of fish and wildlife habitat.

None of these amendments, taken alone or in concert, will guarantee that Colorado River ecosystems will receive the protection they deserve. That will require ambitious and ongoing efforts to use the amendments to change how we manage the river, dams, and infrastructure that have been employed for human uses alone. The amendments would be an essential first step, however, to update the Law of the River to embrace environmental values and interests that have evolved since 1922.

Conclusion

The idea that human management of the Colorado River should reflect environmental as well as human utilitarian values is hardly new. Fittingly, one of the best expressions of this idea comes from the namesake for the Wallace Stegner Lecture. In his essay "Glen Canyon Submersus," published in 1969 as part of *The Sound of Mountain Water*, Stegner critiqued the damming of Glen Canyon:

> Silt pockets out of reach of flood were gardens of fern and redbud; every talus and rockslide gave footing to cottonwood and willow and single-leafed ash; ponded places were solid with watercress; maidenhair hung from seepage cracks in the cliffs.... In gaining the lovely and the usable, we have given up the incomparable.... The wildlife that used to live comfortably in Glen Canyon is not there...this reservoir...leaves no home for beaver or waterbird.

As usual, Stegner got it right. The Colorado is a living river. It is worth more than money, and the law should protect its nonmonetary as well as its monetary values. We can and should change the Law of the River to embrace the environmental values of a new generation.

NOTES

1. I am indebted to the river advocacy group Living Rivers, based in Moab, Utah, for the inspiration to use this terminology.
2. The lecture combines ideas presented in my book *Restoring Colorado Ecosystems: A Troubled Sense of Immensity* (Washington, DC: Island Press, 2007), and in my chapter contribution to Jason Robison's book *Cornerstone: A Century of the Colorado River Compact* (Tucson: University of Arizona Press), with new ideas presented in the Stegner Lecture.
3. Benjamin N. Cardozo, *The Nature of the Judicial Process* (New Haven, CT: Yale University Press, 1921).
4. Roscoe Pound, *Interpretations of Legal History* (Cambridge, MA: Harvard University Press, 1946).
5. Loving v. Virginia, 388 U.S. 1 (1967).
6. See U.S. Const., Amends. XV and XIX.
7. Colorado River Compact, 45 Stat. 1064 (1928).
8. Compact Art. III(c) included a "placeholder" for a potential future treaty with Mexico by specifying how the Upper and Lower Basins would share responsibility for any guaranteed flows to Mexico.
9. The compact granted no water or water rights to Native Americans. Article VII merely provided that nothing in the compact impaired any obligation the federal government might have to tribes in the basin.
10. In a nutshell, the compact apportioned 7.5 million acre-feet (maf) of water for annual beneficial consumptive use in the Upper Basin; the same amount for annual beneficial consumptive use in the Lower Basin, plus an addition 1 maf for use in the Lower Basin if available; and imposed on the Upper Basin a firm delivery obligation to ensure that the Lower Basin received its apportionment regardless of river flows at any point in time, enforced over rolling ten-year periods.
11. Theodore Roosevelt, "First Annual Message to Congress" (December 3, 1901) (emphasis added).
12. John Wesley Powell, "The Lesson of Conemaugh," *The North American Review* 149, no. 393 (1889): 10–56.
13. Treaty Between the United States of America and Mexico respecting Utilization of Waters of the Colorado and Tijuana Rivers and of the Rio Grande, 59 Stat. 1219 (November 8, 1945).
14. The Upper Basin Compact is available at https://www.usbr.gov/lc/region /g1000/pdfiles/ucbsnact.pdf. This is a second interstate agreement

designed to apportion water and Upper Basin obligations under the Colorado River Compact among the Upper Basin states.

15. Pub. L. No. 642–70 (1928).
16. Pub. L. No. 485, ch. 203 (1956).
17. Pub. L. No. 90–537 (1968).
18. Pub. L. No. 102–575 (1992).
19. National Environmental Policy Act of 1969, 42 U.S.C. §4321 et seq.; Endangered Species Act of 1973, 16 U.S.C. §1531 et seq.
20. Nat'l Ass'n of Homebuilders v. Defenders of Wildlife, 551 U.S. 644 (2007).
21. Grand Canyon Trust v. U.S. Bureau of Reclamation, 691 F.3d 1008 (9th Cir. 2012).
22. The All-American Canal replaced an earlier canal through Mexico and back into California, which irrigators viewed as untenable due to political instability in Mexico at the time. Mexico built the Morales Dam to store water delivered at the international border for use by its farms and cities.
23. Since that time, massive dams have been built all around the world, making that assessment challenging. See World Commission on Dams, *Dams and Development: A New Framework for Decision-Making* (November 2000).
24. 86 Fed. Reg. 57588 (October 18, 2021).
25. U.S. Fish and Wildlife Service, "Species Status Assessment for the Humpback Chub (*Gila cypha*)" (March 2018).
26. FWS, "Species Status Assessment."
27. See Bradley Udall and Jonathan Overpeck, "The Twenty-First Century Colorado River Hot Drought and Implications for the Future," *Water Resources Research* 53 (2017): 2404.
28. FWS, "Species Status Assessment."
29. 82 Fed. Reg. 61725 (December 29, 2017).
30. Christopher D. Stone, *Should Trees Have Standing? And Other Essays on Law, Morals and the Environment* (Oceana Publications, 1996). The essay was first published in 45 S. Cal. L. Rev. 450 (1972).
31. Aldo Leopold, "The Land Ethic," in *A Sand County Almanac, with Essays on Conservation from Round River* (New York: Oxford University Press, 1966).
32. U.S. Const., Amends. I—X; United Nations, Universal Declaration on Human Rights (1948).
33. "'Mister!' he said with a sawdusty sneeze, I am the Lorax. I speak for the trees." Dr. Seuss, *The Lorax* (1971).
34. See United Nations, Harmony with Nature, available at http://www .harmonywithnatureun.org/rightsOfNature/ (identifying rights of nature provisions in nations around the world).
35. República del Ecuador [Constitution], October 20, 2008, ch. 7, art. 71.
36. See Global Alliance for the Rights of Nature (GARN), *The First Successful Case of the Rights of Nature Implementation in Ecuador*, (May 21, 2011), https://www.garn.org/first-ron-case-ecuador/.